ADVENTURES IN
MEMORY™

"Mrs. Riley Bought Five Itchy Aardvarks"

and Other Painless Tricks for Memorizing Science Facts

BRIAN P. CLEARY

Illustrated by **J. P. SANDY**

M Millbrook Press · Minneapolis

To my daughter Grace
—B.P.C.

To Joyce, Eric, and Michael
—J.P.S.

Text copyright © 2008 by Brian P. Cleary
Illustrations copyright © 2008 by Lerner Publishing Group, Inc.

Millbrook Press
A division of Lerner Publishing Group, Inc.
241 First Avenue North
Minneapolis, MN 55401 U.S.A.

Website address: www.lernerbooks.com

Library of Congress Cataloging-in-Publication Data

Cleary, Brian P., 1959-
     "Mrs. Riley Bought Five Itchy Aardvarks" and other painless tricks for
memorizing science facts / by Brian P. Cleary ; illustrated by J. P. Sandy.
          p.   cm. — (Adventures in memory)
     Includes index.
     ISBN 978-0-8225-7819-2 (lib. bdg. : alk. paper)
     1. Science—Study and teaching (Elementary)—Audio-visual aids. 2. Mnemonics—
Juvenile literature. 3. Scientific recreations—Juvenile literature. I. Sandy, J. P., ill.
II. Title.
     Q190.C57 2008
     372.35'044—dc22   2007052125

Manufactured in the United States of America
1 2 3 4 5 6 - DP - 13 12 11 10 09 08

HOW THIS BOOK WILL HELP YOU MEMORIZE SCIENCE FACTS

Mnemonic
(pronounced *nih-MAH-nik*)

is a fancy word given to little tricks or devices that help us memorize important facts. Some of them rhyme, such as,

> "Columbus sailed the ocean blue in fourteen-hundred-ninety-two."

Other memory aids build a word made up of the first letters of a list we're trying to memorize. **HOMES** is a trick for remembering the names of the five great lakes (**H**uron, **O**ntario, **M**ichigan, **E**rie, and **S**uperior). The word HOMES contains the first letter of the name of each lake.

Still other memory tools are more visual, meaning that a picture will help us to remember a fact, such as this one: **A Bactrian camel has a back shaped like the letter "B" turned on its side. A Dromedary camel has a back shaped like the letter "D" turned on its side.** So we know a Bactrian camel has two humps and a Dromedary camel has one.

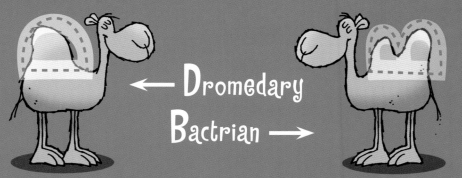

← Dromedary

Bactrian →

In this book, you'll find lots of fun ways to memorize science facts. But what I'm really hoping is that you'll develop your own tricks. Oftentimes the words, silly rhymes, or crazy sentences that you invent will be the most meaningful way for you to master science!

Here's an example of what I thought of to memorize the six major animal groups: **Mrs. Riley Bought Five Itchy Aardvarks.** That stands for: **Mammals, Reptiles, Birds, Fish, Insects, Amphibians**. But let's say your principal's name is Mr. Robbins. It might be more meaningful (and therefore memorable) for you to say:

Mr. Robbins Barfed Five Icky Apples.

Sometimes, it's the absurd nature of what you've come up with that will help you to remember. They say that **elephants never forget**. Well, now that you know about mnemonics, neither will you!

SPACE IS THE PLACE

The planets in our solar system in order from the Sun are:

Mercury Venus Earth Mars

Mel's Very Excited Ma

Jupiter

Saturn

Uranus

Neptune

Just Served Us Nachos

EXTRA CREDIT

Scientists used to think that Pluto was a planet. In 2006 they decided it should be called a dwarf planet instead. Dwarf planets are smaller than true planets. Scientists have found three dwarf planets so far, but they expect to find many more.

WHAT GOES AROUND

The word **orbit** means "revolves around." If you circle around a soccer ball, you're orbiting it. Visualize these pictures when you need to remember what goes around what. Be careful not to get dizzy!

Earth orbits the Sun.

The Moon orbits Earth.

EXTRA CREDIT

Earth makes one full orbit around the Sun every 365.25 days. The Moon makes one full orbit around Earth every 27.3 days.

H-2-OH, IS THAT A FACT?

H_2O is the chemical formula for water. It tells us that a molecule of water contains two hydrogen (H) atoms and one oxygen (O) atom.

Knowing the difference between freshwater and salt water is easy. Freshwater is not salty. Salt water is salty. When you need to know the facts about water, just think of these pictures.

Most of Earth is covered with water.

Most of that water is salt water.

glacier

river

lake

Think of this picture to remember that **freshwater** comes from **glaciers, rivers,** and **lakes,** and think of the fish wearing <u>underwear</u> to remember it also comes from <u>**underground sources.**</u>

FRESHWATER HERE!

underground source

READ ON!
Learn about the water cycle in the book *Why Does It Rain?* by Judith Jango-Cohen.

GEOLOGY ROCKS!

(... and speaking of rocks, let's talk about the three types)

A RHYME ABOUT IGNEOUS ROCK

This type of rock is
formed when the lava

(a zillion times hotter
than cocoa or java)

from a volcano is
cooled over time.

Whenever you need to,
remember this rhyme.

Hear: Igneous, **think** ignite, which has to do with fire. Then picture a volcano with hot lava flowing out of it. It may also help when you hear **lava** to think of java (hot coffee) to connect the two hot liquids in your mind!

examples of igneous rock: granite, pumice, basalt, and obsidian

A RHYME ABOUT **SEDIMENTARY ROCK**

Formed when the sediment, gravel, and sand
settle, collecting in lakes and on land.
In rivers or seas, they're cemented together
over millions of years both by time and by weather.

Hear: Sedimentary, **think** sand, or settle. Or better yet, learn the word **sediment**. It refers to the stuff that settles to the bottom of something liquid, like in certain types of salad dressing or in Kool-Aid that has too much drink mix in it. Sedimentary rocks are formed from sediment. These rocks cover about three-fourths of the surface of the continents.

examples of sedimentary rock: sandstone, limestone, and shale

A RHYME ABOUT METAMORPHIC ROCK

Metamorphic rocks
have changed,

by pressure or
by heat.

Remember this
when tested,

and your score
will not be beat.

Hear: Metamorphic, **think** metamorphosis, which has to do with change, as in a caterpillar changing into a butterfly. Picture that change, and remember that metamorphic rocks have been transformed, or changed, from igneous, sedimentary, or other metamorphic rocks.

examples of metamorphic rock: marble, schist, slate, and gneiss

READ ON!
Find out more by reading
Rocks by Sally M. Walker.

HARD & SOFT

The Mohs hardness scale lists ten minerals in order from soft to hard. They are **Talc**, **Gypsum**, **Calcite**, **Fluorite**, **Apatite**, **Orthoclase Feldspar**, **Quartz**, **Topaz**, **Corundum**, and **Diamond**. Geologists use the minerals on this scale to help identify unknown minerals.

**Talking Guppies
Can Fluster
An Old
Quiet Toad
Called Diana**

BLAH BLAH BLAH BLAH BLAH BLAH

SMALL CHANGE

Three processes slowly change Earth's surface. Water can play a part in each one. To remember them, think of **DEW**, which is made of water.

D for Deposition: dropping off soil, rocks, and sand that were carried away by erosion. Rivers often deposit soil where they flow into lakes or oceans.

E for Erosion: the movement of rock, soil, and other bits of earth. Wind, water, and ice cause erosion.

W for Weathering: breaking rocks and soil into smaller pieces. Ice, water, and growing plants cause weathering.

READ ON!

Do you want to make sure that your knowledge of erosion doesn't erode? Read *Erosion* by Joelle Riley.

SKYWRITING

A Rhyme about Clouds

Cumulus, cirrus, nimbus and stratus . . . answer the cloud questions teachers throw at us.

Stratus clouds cover the sky so you can't see the Sun. They are low and gray.

Cirrus clouds are thin and wispy. They are very high in the sky.

Cumulus clouds are flat on the bottom and fluffy on top. They often mean good weather.

Nimbus clouds mean rain, and they come in two forms. *Cumulonimbus* clouds often bring thunderstorms. And *nimbostratus* clouds are low, gray clouds that bring rain.

WHAT'S THE MATTER?

Solid, Liquid, or Gas—That's What!   A Rhyme about Matter

Matter is anything that takes up space and can be weighed. Solids, liquids, and gases are the three states of matter on Earth.

Whether you hold it
or mold it or spin it.
Whether you drink it
or mix something in it.
Everything everywhere's
one of these things:
a **SOLID**, a **LIQUID**, or **GAS**.

Whether it's floating
or streaming or gleaming.
Whether it's shedding
or spreading or steaming.

Everything everywhere's
one of these things:
a **SOLID**, a **LIQUID**, or **GAS**.

If it's the ocean,
some potion, or lotion,
and if it should move
in a flowing-like motion,
this is a LIQUID,
so stick with me now:
it isn't a SOLID or GAS.

If it's some wood
or some plastic or stone,
keeping its shape
when you leave it alone,
this is a SOLID,
so follow me now:
it isn't a GAS or a LIQUID.

That leaves us gas,
which we often can't see:
like Freon and neon and
air to name three.
It won't split or splatter
'cause GAS is the matter
that isn't a LIQUID or SOLID!

READ ON!
Why does matter matter? Find
out by doing the experiments in
Matter by Sally M. Walker.

HOT & COLD

The boiling point of water is 212° Fahrenheit (F) and 100° Celsius (C).
The freezing point of water is 32° Fahrenheit (F) and 0° Celsius (C).

212°F | 100°C

Mr. Fahrenheit is boiling 212 hot dogs.

Mrs. Celsius is boiling 100 hot dogs.

Mr. Fahrenheit has 32 snow cones in his freezer.

32°F 0°C

Mrs. Celsius has 0 snow cones in her freezer.

EXTRA CREDIT

In 1724 Daniel Gabriel Fahrenheit created the Fahrenheit system for measuring temperature. In 1742 Anders Celsius created the Celsius system. The United States is one of only a few countries that uses the Fahrenheit system.

LiGHT

by Dr. Ray
from the CD: *Three Things*
Permanent Records

Have you ever wanted to do a rap in school? Here's your chance! Have one person read the first two lines of every stanza out loud. The rest of the class will say the third line together. By the end, I guarantee you'll never forget the three things light can do!

When light reaches somethin'
like a pool or a pumpkin:
reflected, refracted, absorbed.

Listen close to my rappin'—
only three things can happen:
reflected, refracted, absorbed.

Just three possibilities,
no need to have ya ill at ease:
reflected, refracted, absorbed.

So don't let it fool ya,
cuz I'm here to school ya:
reflected, refracted, absorbed.

When light hits an object,
like a door or a knob, check:
reflected, refracted, absorbed.

No need to have a showdown,
one of three things will go down:
reflected, refracted, absorbed.

Not five, six, or seven,
cuz here's the four-eleven:
reflected, refracted, absorbed.

It isn't subliminal,
hard core, or criminal:
reflected, refracted, absorbed.

If you whisper or shout, come
and tell me the outcome:
reflected, refracted, absorbed.

You can't disrespect it,
dismiss or reject it:
reflected, refracted, absorbed.

MORE LIGHT RAP

The smart ones detect it
on a test, they select it:
reflected, refracted, absorbed.

When an object and light meet,
remember, get it right, Pete:
reflected, refracted, absorbed.

They're all up in your grill?
Take a deep breath and chill:
reflected, refracted, absorbed.

Cuz the answer's a breeze
when you're holding the keys:
reflected, refracted, absorbed.

Only three things occur,
when this happens, for sure:
reflected, refracted, absorbed.

Not four, five, or six—
light has only three tricks:
reflected, refracted, absorbed.

Word.

These stanzas will help you remember the meaning of **reflected**, **refracted**, and **absorbed**.

REFLECTED
When light hits something shiny,
whether fat or tall or tiny:
the light's gonna be reflected.

REFRACTED
When the light hits some water,
listen up, my son and daughter,
the light is always refracted.

ABSORBED
When a color's hit by light,
that color may look bright,
but the light is being absorbed.

EXTRA CREDIT
reflect = bounce off
refract = bend
absorb = soak up

THE CLASSIFICATION STATION

Scientists put all living things, including plants and animals, into many groups. This grouping is known as classification. Classification helps explain how living things are related to one another. Kingdom is the biggest group, and species is the smallest. Here are the seven major categories used to classify living things:

Kingdom, Phylum, Class, Order, Family, Genus, Species

King Philip Climbed Over

Furry Green Spiders

WHAT A BUNCH OF ANIMALS!

The six major animal groups are:

Mammals

Reptiles

Birds

Fish

Insects

Amphibians

EXTRA CREDIT

What exactly is an animal? It's an organism that is made from many cells, can move on its own, and gets food by eating other organisms.

DOWN AT THE RECYCLING PLANT

A Play about the Ecosystem

You know those corny school plays where somebody has to dress up as a sunflower or a rutabaga? Of course, you do! You're still in school! Let's pretend we're putting on a play about the ecosystem.

An ecosystem is a kind of community. But instead of a community of people, it's a community of plants and animals and their environment.

This girl—we'll call her **Sarah**—is going to play the part of the **Sun**. The Sun is the source of all energy in our ecosystem. You see, it provides the light that plants need to live and grow. It also keeps everything warm so all the plants and animals don't freeze to death! Without the Sun, we wouldn't have an ecosystem at all. Sarah doesn't have any lines. She'll just stand here and beam her sunny Sarah smile. Radiant, isn't she?

What else does our ecosystem need? All the plants and animals need water to survive. Scientists call water **H₂O** because it's two parts hydrogen and one part oxygen. **Holly** will be the first hydrogen, and **Haley** will be the second **hydrogen**. **Omar** will be the **oxygen**. These three will wear blue shirts and join hands. They'll move flowingly across the stage and make whooshing and gurgling sounds, like water.

Next up is air. Air contains a gas called oxygen and a gas called carbon dioxide. Without oxygen, animals (including us!) couldn't breathe. And without carbon dioxide, plants would all die. So these two, **Erin** and **Aaron**, will play the **air**. They'll slowly move their hands up and down and walk around. Since air is hard to see, they can carry a clear shower curtain.

If we want plants here, we need somewhere for plants to grow. How about some soil? **Sophia**, **Michael**, and **Nikko** can handle this role. Their first names begin with *s*, *m*, and *n* to remind us of **soil**, and the **minerals** and **nutrients** in the soil. They'll wear brown T-shirts and use cheerleading megaphones to urge the plants to

"G-R-O-W . . . what's that spell?"

Plants are what's known in ecosystem-speak as **producers**. (Think of the produce section at the grocery store if that helps—it's kind of green and leafy there.) Producers produce their own energy thanks to photosynthesis. **Pedro**, **Patrick**, and **Padma** are the plants in this play. Note the green T-shirts on this trio. They will crouch down and then slowly stand up and reach their hands skyward, showing how they're growing.

Consumers eat producers. Our consumers, **Conrad** and **Connie**, will make chomping motions with their arms as they move close to the plants. Some consumers also eat other consumers, but that's a little too violent for our play!

Finally, here are **DeShawn** and **Denise**, two **decomposers**. What would happen if all the producers and consumers didn't decay (yes, that means rot!) when they died? We'd have miles of piles, wouldn't we? Our decomposers are using karate chops to break down everything around them. Decomposers are usually fungi and bacteria. They break down dead animals and plants and turn them into minerals and nutrients. (Michael and Nikko— quick—get over here!) Decom- posers are like nature's little recycling station. That's why Denise and DeShawn both have recycling T-shirts on!

Let's hear it for Sun, water, air, soil, minerals, nutrients, producers, consumers, and decomposers. Without them, we'd have nothing to cheer about!

THAT'S NOT HARD TO SWALLOW!

The Seven Steps of Digestion

What are the seven steps of digestion in order? To remember, look at the first two letters in each of the words on the next page:

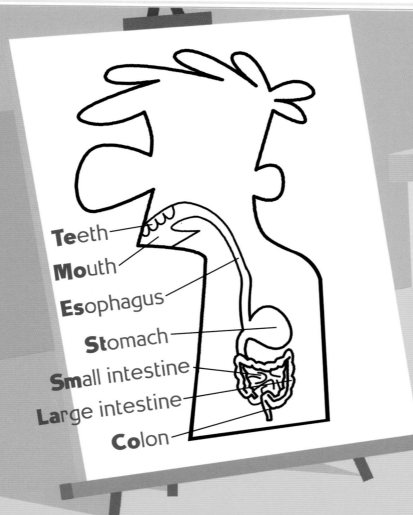

Teeth
Mouth
Esophagus
Stomach
Small intestine
Large intestine
Colon

Ted's Mouse, Esther, Stayed Small, Laughing Continuously

READ ON:
Do you want to see photos of the digestive system in action? Look for *The Digestive System* by Rebecca L. Johnson.

A Very Silly Song about PHOTOSYNTHESIS

Photosynthesis is how plants make their own food. Without it, we wouldn't have plants. And animals and humans couldn't live without plants—or the oxygen they make for us to breathe.

WATER

SUNLIGHT

CARBON DIOXIDE

OXYGEN

CARBOHYDRATES

CARBOHYDRATES

For photosynthesis, a plant needs sunlight, water, and carbon dioxide from the air. The plant uses these things to make carbohydrates and oxygen. The carbohydrates feed the plant. The oxygen goes back into the air. Chloroplasts are tiny structures inside plants that make photosynthesis happen. They make the carbohydrates and oxygen. Chlorophyll is another structure inside plants. It helps with photosynthesis by soaking up sunlight. It also gives plants their green color.

Here's a fun and goofy way for you to remember some of the major terms in the process of photosynthesis. Sing this to the tune of "Row, Row, Row Your Boat."

Pho-to-syn-the-sis
helps us all to thrive.
Animals, plants, and people too—
it keeps us all alive!

Carbon di-ox-ide
is everywhere you go.
Plants receive it from the air,
and it's what helps them grow.

Plants need water too
and bright light from the Sun.
They make car-bo-hy-drates, and
then they're almost done.

Chlor-o-plasts are where
all this change is made.
And chlor-o-phyll's the reason why
the plants have their green shade.

Ox-y-gen is formed
from these plants as well.
This is photosynthesis—
there's nothing more to tell!

THE SCIENCE OF SCIENCE

When scientists have a question, they go through several steps to find the answer. They are: **observation**, **question**, **hypothesis**, **prediction**, **experiment**, **analysis**, and **decision**. These steps are called the scientific method. Here, we'll walk through each of the steps to learn about a stinky problem for the students in Room 113.

OBSERVATION: On certain days, the students of Room 113 notice a funny smell in their classroom. The smell is a mixture of expired yogurt, cheap foot cream, dandruff, old ham, and toupee glue. The smell seems to appear every time Mr. Ebertsonlington is the substitute teacher.

QUESTION: Could the smell be coming from Mr. Ebertsonlington?

HYPOTHESIS: This is another word for "educated guess." The hypothesis here is that the smell IS coming from Mr. Ebertsonlington.

PREDICTION: On days that Mr. Ebertsonlington is NOT teaching in this classroom, the class will return to its normal smell of gerbil food and window cleaner. AHHH! That would smell like roses right about now!

EXPERIMENT: The "real" teacher of Room 113, Mrs. Funkadellic, will be gone Monday of one week, Wednesday of the following week, and Friday of the week after that. Mr. Ebertsonlington is scheduled to sub. If the smell returns on all three days, it would mean that Mr. Ebertsonlington could, indeed, be the source of the smell.

The students of Room 113 make a plan to collect data (a word that means "information") about the smell of the classroom for the next three weeks.

Here is the chart they used to record the data:

DATE	TEACHER*	SMELL IN CLASSROM	
			Week One
April 3	Mr. E.	expired yogurt, cheap foot cream, dandruff, old ham, and toupee glue	
April 4	Mrs. F	gerbil food and window cleaner	
April 5	Mrs. F	gerbil food and window cleaner	
April 6	Mrs. F	gerbil food and window cleaner	
April 7	Mrs. F	gerbil food and window cleaner	
			Week Two
April 10	Mrs. F	gerbil food and window cleaner	
April 11	Mrs. F	gerbil food and window cleaner	
April 12	Mr. E.	expired yogurt, cheap foot cream, dandruff, old ham, and toupee glue	
April 13	Mrs. F	gerbil food and window cleaner	
April 14	Mrs. F	gerbil food and window cleaner	
			Week Three
April 17	Mrs. F	gerbil food and window cleaner	
April 18	Mrs. F	gerbil food and window cleaner	
April 19	Mrs. F	gerbil food and window cleaner	
April 20	Mrs. F	gerbil food and window cleaner	
April 21	Mr. E.	expired yogurt, cheap foot cream, dandruff, old ham, and toupee glue	

*Mr. E.=Mr. Ebertsonlington Mrs. F=Mrs. Funkadellic

ANALYSIS: The data seem to show that Mr. Ebertsonlington is the source of the awful smell. But good scientists also check for other ways to explain their data. Suppose the custodian always cleans the classroom the night before Mr. Ebertsonlington teaches. Then the smell might come from a cleaner made from expired yogurt, cheap foot cream, dandruff, old ham, and toupee glue that he uses to wash down the room. The students ask the custodian when he cleans. He cleans every Saturday. So he can't be causing the smell. Just to be sure, the students ask to smell the cleaner he uses. Wow—that's some powerful window cleaner! The students check for other things that might explain their data. They can't come up with anything else.

DECISION: It's time to say that we either reject our hypothesis or say that we cannot reject our hypothesis. Those are the only two choices! Here are the things the students know:

- **The smell returned on each of Mr. Ebertsonlington's three visits.**

- **Each of Mr. Ebertsonlington's visits were many days apart.**

- **They have not found another way to explain what's causing the smell.**

The students decide that they cannot reject their hypothesis. Note that they didn't PROVE the hypothesis. They simply could not REJECT the hypothesis based on the steps they went through. That's as much "proof positive" as you get in true scientific experiment. They're still pretty sure where the smell came from, however.

EXTRA CREDIT

What if one day when Mr. Ebertsonlington taught, the classroom smelled like gerbil food and window cleaner? Then the students would have had to reject their hypothesis and come up with a new one.

EXTRA EXTRA CREDIT

Find out how to set up your own science experiment at this website: http://school.discoveryeducation.com/sciencefaircentral/scifairstudio/handbook/scientificmethod.html.

GLOSSARY

absorb: light that is absorbed is soaked up by an object. (*see* pp. 24-27)

amphibians: cold-blooded animals with backbones. When they are young, they live in water and breathe through gills. When they are adults, they live on land and breathe through lungs. (*see* p. 30)

birds: warm-blooded animals with backbones that lay eggs and have feathers and wings (*see* p. 30)

carbohydrates: a type of food that provides energy. Plants make carbohydrates. (*see* pp. 38-39)

carbon dioxide: a gas in the air. Plants need it to live. (*see* pp. 33, 38-39)

cells: the smallest units of life. Cells are the building blocks of living things. (*see* p. 30)

Celsius: a scale for measuring temperature. Water freezes at 0°C. Water boils at 100°C. (*see* pp. 22-33)

chlorophyll: a substance in plants that soaks up sunlight. It gives plants their green color. (*see* pp. 38-39)

chloroplasts: tiny structures in plants that make photosynthesis happen (*see* pp. 38-39)

cirrus: clouds that are thin and wispy (*see* pp. 18-19)

classification: grouping all living things to explain how they are related to one another (*see* pp. 28-29)

consumer: in an ecosystem, an organism that cannot produce its own food. Animals are consumers. Consumers eat producers and other consumers to get food. (*see* pp. 34-35)

cumulus: clouds that are flat on the bottom and fluffy on top (*see* pp. 18-19)

decay: to rot or break down (*see* p. 35)

deposition: when soil, rocks, and sand carried away by erosion are dropped off (*see* pp. 16-17)

digestion: breaking down food so the body can use it (*see* pp. 38-39)

ecosystem: a community of plants and animals and the environment in which they live (*see* pp. 32-35)

erosion: the movement of rock, soil, and other bits of earth (*see* pp. 16-17)

Fahrenheit: a scale for measuring temperature. Water freezes at 32°F. Water boils at 212°F. (*see* pp. 22-23)

fish: cold-blooded animals with backbones that live in water, breathe through gills, and have scales (*see* p. 30)

freshwater: water that does not contain salt. Rivers, glaciers, underwater sources, and most lakes contain freshwater. (*see* p. 10)

gas: a substance such as air. A gas can spread out to fill any container. (*see* pp. 21-22, 33)

geology: the scientific study of Earth and Earth's rocks and minerals (*see* pp. 12-16)

H₂O: the chemical formula for water (*see* pp. 10-11, 33)

hypothesis: an educated guess about how an experiment will turn out (*see* pp. 40-44)

igneous rock: rock formed from volcanic lava that has cooled (*see* p. 12)

insects: animals without backbones that have three pairs of legs, wings, three body parts, and an exoskeleton (*see* p. 30)

liquid: a substance that flows easily. A liquid always stays the same size, but its shape can change. (*see* pp. 20-21)

mammals: warm-blooded animals that have backbones, breathe air, and produce milk for their young (*see* p. 30)

matter: anything that takes up space and can be weighed (*see* pp. 20-21)

metamorphic rock: formed from other rocks that have been changed by pressure or heat (*see* p. 14)

minerals: natural substances that mix together to make rocks. Minerals also help plants grow. (*see* pp. 15, 34-35)

Mohs hardness scale: a list of ten minerals that helps scientists identify unknown minerals (*see* p. 15)

nimbus: clouds that bring rain (*see* pp. 18-19)

nutrients: substances that plants and animals need to grow (*see* pp. 34-35)

orbit: to travel in an invisible path around the Sun, a star, a planet, or other heavenly body (*see* pp. 8-9)

oxygen: a chemical in the air that people and animals need to breathe (*see* pp. 10-11, 33, 38-39)

photosynthesis: the process by which plants make food for themselves. They take water, carbon dioxide, and sunlight and make carbohydrates and oxygen. (*see* pp. 34, 38-39)

planets: large objects that orbit stars. Our solar system has eight planets. (*see* pp. 6-7)

producers: in an ecosystem, an organism that can produce its own food. Plants are producers. (*see* pp. 34-35)

reflect: light that is reflected bounces off an object (*see* pp. 24-27)

refract: light that is refracted bends when it passes from one material to another (*see* pp. 24-27)

reptiles: cold-blooded animals that have backbones and scaly skin, breathe air, and lay eggs (*see* p. 30)

rocks: hard natural substances made from minerals (*see* pp. 12-14)

rutabaga: a vegetable with a pale yellow root that can be eaten (*see* p. 32)

salt water: salty water that is found in oceans, seas, and some other bodies of water, such as the Great Salt Lake in Utah (*see* pp. 10-11)

scientific method: the process scientists use to run experiments and make discoveries (*see* pp. 40-44)

sedimentary rock: formed from layers of sediment that are pressed tightly together (*see* p. 13)

soil: minerals and other substances on Earth's surface. Plants grow in soil. (*see* pp. 16-17, 34-35)

solar system: the sun and all the heavenly bodies that orbit around it. These bodies include planets, moons, asteroids, and comets. (*see* pp. 6-7)

solid: a substance that stays the same size and the same shape. Wood is a solid. (*see* pp. 20-21)

stratus: clouds that are low and gray (*see* pp. 18-19)

weathering: breaking rocks and soil into smaller pieces (*see* pp. 16-17)

READ ON!

BOOKS

Jango-Cohen, Judith. *Why Does It Rain?* Minneapolis: Millbrook Press, 2006.

Johnson, Rebecca L. *The Digestive System.* Minneapolis: Lerner Publications Company, 2005.

Riley, Joelle. *Erosion.* Minneapolis: Lerner Publications Company, 2007.

Walker, Sally M. *Matter.* Minneapolis: Lerner Publications Company, 2006.

Walker, Sally M. *Rocks.* Minneapolis: Lerner Publications Company, 2007.

WEBSITES

Biology 4 Kids
http://www.biology4kids.com
Follow the links on this site to learn more about plants, animals, and cells.

How Rocks Are Formed
http://www.rocksforkids.com/RFK/howrocks.html
Read about rocks, minerals, crystals, soil, erosion, the rock cycle, and more.

Howstuffworks "Physical Science Channel"
http://science.howstuffworks.com/physical-science-channel.htm
This website explains the science behind everything from hot air balloons and microscopes to cameras and contact lenses.

How the Body Works
http://www.kidshealth.org/kidhtbw/htbw_main_page.html
Learn more about your organs and body systems. This website includes lots of fun diagrams.

Science@NASA—Science Fun and Games
http://science.hq.nasa.gov/kids/index.html
The National Aeronautics and Space Administration has a special website for kids. It has information about NASA, Earth, the Sun, the solar system, and the universe.

INDEX